KT-132-971

Robert Bruce:

Cover picture: Statue of Robert Bruce at Bannockburn.
Inside cover picture: The Pass of Brander, Argyll.
Above: Bruce's Stone at Glen Trool.

Text based on *Bruce's Scotland* by Mari Spankie, published by Wayland in 1994.

First published in 1995 by Wayland (Publishers) Ltd,
61 Western Road, Hove, East Sussex, BN3 1JD, England.

British Library Cataloguing in Publication Data
Stephen, Margaret
Robert Bruce: Scotland's Hero King
I. Title
941.102092

ISBN 0 7502 1547 x

Consultants: Donald Gunn, Education Officer for BBC Scotland, and Mari Spankie.
Editor: Katrina Maitland Smith
Book design: Pardoe Blacker Limited
Typesetting: Steve Wheele Design
Printed and bound by B.P.C. Paulton Books, Great Britain

To the reader:
This is an information book. You may wish to read it from beginning to end, but you may choose only to read certain pages to answer your questions or to find the information you require. Don't forget to look at the pictures. They work with the words to tell you about Robert Bruce and the Scotland of his time.

To the teacher:
Most benefit will be derived from this text if pupils are introduced to the topic and its specialized vocabulary before reading takes place. Where background knowledge has been gleaned from related materials, such as television and radio programmes, young people will be in a better position not only to use books to find information they require but also to pose their own questions.

Group discussion sessions provide a worthwhile introduction to the information book. Initial examination of layout, illustration and text in the group situation will provide individuals with the confidence to access information.
This text can be used alongside the original to ensure that all pupils have the opportunity to read and learn.

Scotland's Hero King

Contents

1 Scotland: many Languages, one Nation 6
2 A Kingdom at Peace 8
3 Trade and the Burghs 10
4 The Scottish Church in the Middle Ages 12
5 1286, King Alexander III 14
6 The Kingdom without a King 16
7 England's Warrior King 18
8 King John Balliol and the Sack of Berwick 20
9 The Rise of William Wallace and Andrew Murray 22
10 Wallace is Defeated 24
11 Murder: a Step to the Throne 26
12 Bruce is Defeated and in Despair 28
13 Civil War 30
14 The Campaign to free the Castles 32
15 The Battle of Bannockburn 34
16 Good King Robert 36
17 The Declaration of Arbroath 38
18 The Bruce Legacy 40
Glossary 42
Further Information 44
Index 45

Scotland: many Languages, one Nation

Robert Bruce was born at Turnberry Castle, on the Ayrshire coast, in the year 1274.

At that time in Scotland several languages were spoken. As Bruce grew up he would hear people speaking Gaelic, Inglis and Norman-French.

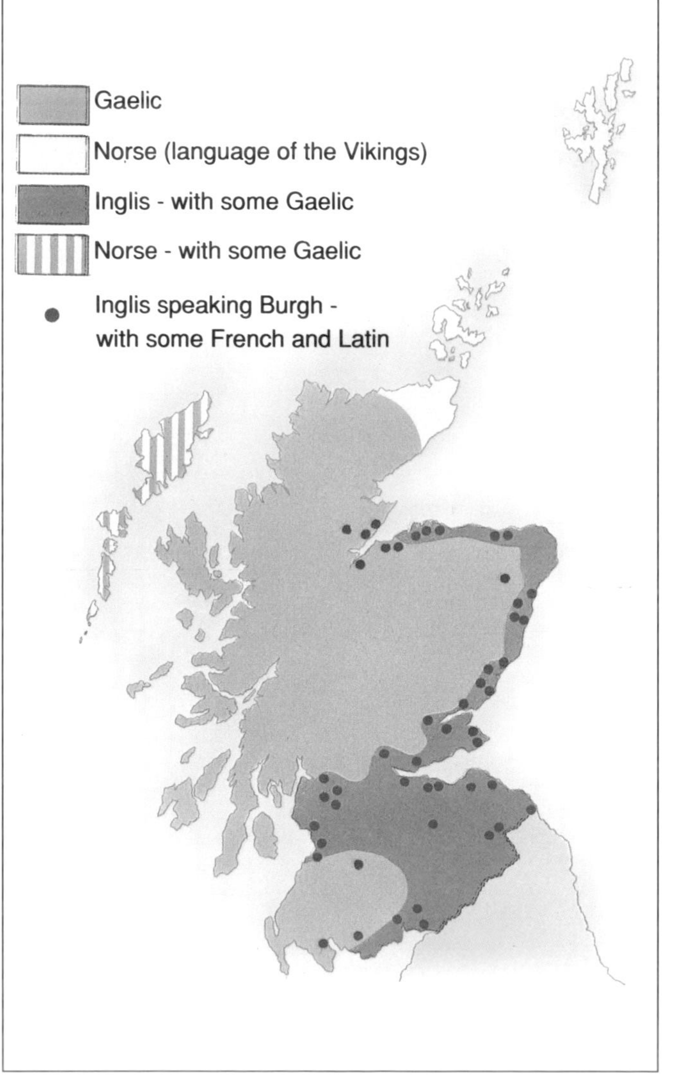

Gaelic

The Gaelic language was spoken by Celtic peoples in Scotland, Ireland and the Isle of Man. Bruce's mother and her family spoke Gaelic, and so did Bruce.

Inglis

In the towns and in the south of Scotland the main language was Inglis, introduced from England. Gradually, Inglis took over from Gaelic as the main language spoken throughout lowland Scotland. Today, many people call this language Scots. Scots used to be the name Inglis-speakers used for Gaelic.

Norman-French

England had been conquered by the Normans in 1066. From that time, Norman-French was spoken by the English kings and nobles. Before David I became King of Scots, he lived in England and spent time at the English king's court.

◀ This map of Scotland shows where the most common languages were spoken in 1300.

King David invited Norman knights, who were good soldiers, to help him rule his kingdom in Scotland. They promised to support the king in exchange for land. They brought their French language with them.

The father of Robert Bruce was a Norman from one of the most powerful families in both England and Scotland. Robert Bruce would learn French from his father and would be trained as a Norman lord.

▲ King David I and his grandson Malcolm IV, from a charter giving lands to Kelso Abbey in 1159. Charters were written in Latin, the language of Church and government.

▲ In the year 1305, a Norman-Scottish family replaced the wooden castle at Duffus with this stone castle and wall.

Bruce's mother came from an important Celtic family. Bruce was able to bring together the separate languages and peoples of Scotland to build a strong nation.

A Kingdom at Peace

Under King Alexander III, Scotland was at peace. Most people lived in touns, little groups of farms, often near a lord's castle. The owner of the castle had between ten and twenty touns on his estate. He collected rents from these touns.

The farmers grew crops, mainly of barley and oats, on the sloping hillsides. They did not know how to drain the flat, wet land. They sold the wool and hides from their sheep and cattle.

▼ An estate around a castle.

Population

- It is estimated that the population of Scotland was nearly 1 million by the year 1300.
- England's population was between 5 and 6 million at this time.
- At least 90 per cent of Scots lived in small rural communities.
- Half the population lived north of the line between the Rivers Clyde and Tay.

Money

- Scottish money was worth the same as English money.
- Scotland had 30-45 million silver pennies in use.

▼ A knight in armour.

Knights were soldiers, not farmers. A knight needed expensive horses, armour and weapons, and depended on rents from tenants to pay for them.

In times of war, tenants followed their knight to fight for the king. These men made up the foot soldiers and archers of the king's army, while the knights formed the cavalry.

In the west, galleys and oarsmen were provided for the king instead of horsemen.

When Robert Bruce was a boy, his family had strong, stone castles and much land in both Scotland and England. They were important nobles. Many people fought for the Bruces in return for land.

Trade and the Burghs

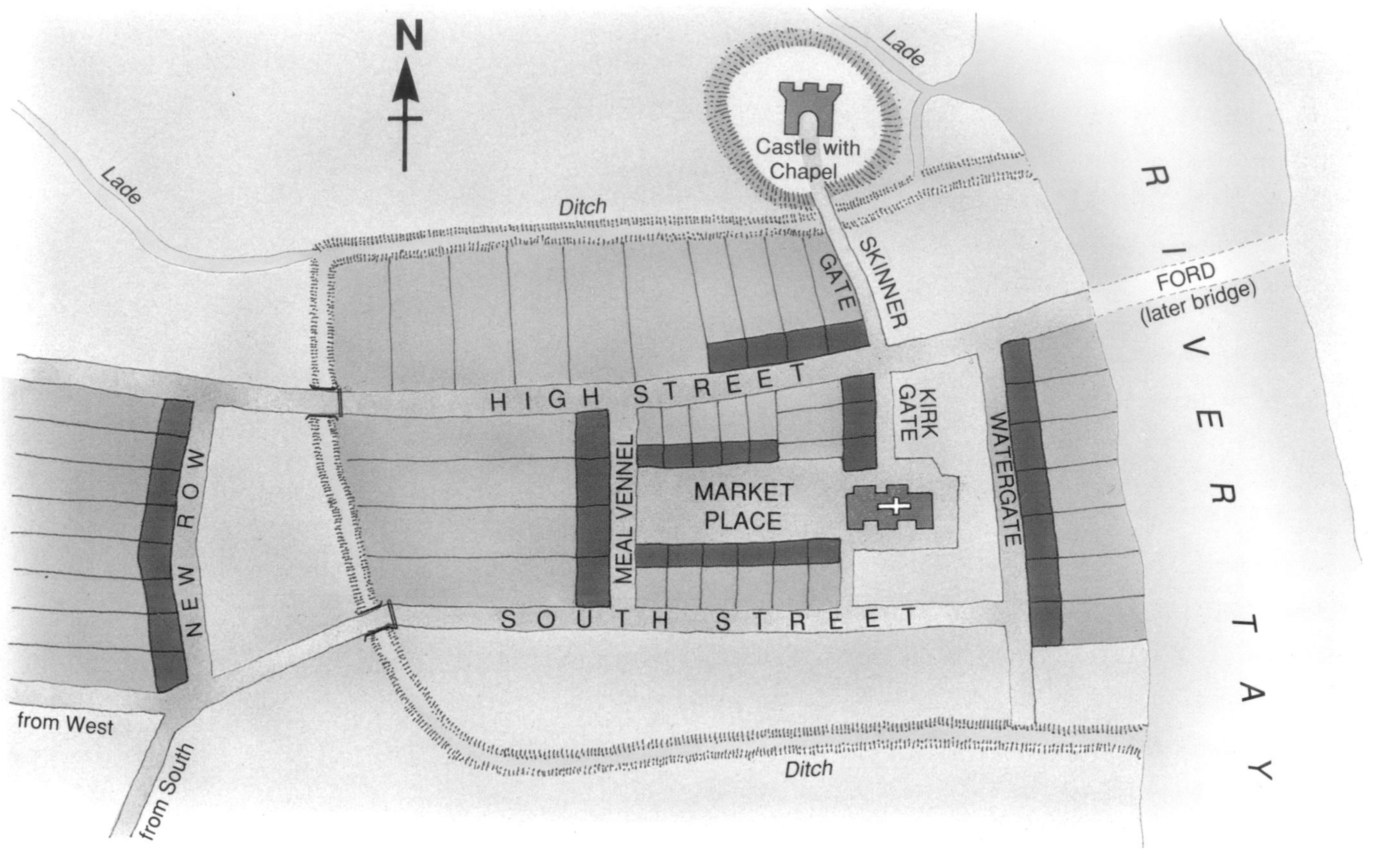

▲ A plan of St. John's Town. We now call it Perth.

The earliest towns in Scotland were set up by kings and called royal burghs. Later, barons set up burghs around their castles. The Bruce family set up their own burgh at Annan.

Markets and fairs took place in the burghs. Farmers had to pay tolls to bring their wool, hides and food into the burghs.

Craftsmen such as weavers, bakers and shoemakers made goods for sale.

The craftsmen's guilds set the prices and checked the quality of goods.

The laws of the burghs were strict. Some people from the burghs were so important that the king listened to their advice.

The most important burghs, such as Aberdeen and Berwick, were on the east coast. Berwick was the richest town in Scotland because the Berwick merchants brought in fine wools to sell to England and other countries in Europe. In return they bought in luxuries like wine and spices.

For their time, burghs were busy places but they were also dangerous and dirty, with rubbish lying everywhere.

People got their water from wells, and there was much disease. Houses were built of wood. They caught fire and burned down easily.

When Alexander III was king (1249-1286), Scotland was at peace for much of the time and trade was helping to improve people's lives.

This picture shows the remains of Roxburgh Castle. ▼

The Scottish Church in the Middle Ages

King David I (1084-1153) helped the church to become very important in Scotland. He gave large amounts of land for monks to set up monasteries and abbeys.

Although there were different orders of monks, they were all expected to live a life of prayer and study. They were expected to work in the fields and, because they worked hard, the abbeys became very wealthy.

In Bruce's time, there were 30 abbeys, 27 priories, 9 nunneries and 20 friaries in Scotland. There were also parish churches all over the country.

The Scottish Church linked people throughout the country, but there were also links with Europe through the Roman Catholic Church. King David had brought Roman Catholic churchmen to Scotland, and their traditions became an important part of the early Celtic Church.

In early days, Christianity was brought to Scotland by missionaries who led very simple lives. St. Columba (Columcille) landed on Iona in 563 and set up the Celtic Church there. ▼

Melrose Abbey was a wealthy abbey in the south of Scotland. Its wool was sent to Berwick to be sold abroad. ▶

Another of the great Scottish abbeys was Kelso Abbey. ▼

Younger sons of noble families often became churchmen and, indeed, Bruce's brother, Alexander, became a clergyman.

Bishops were powerful churchmen and often took part in the king's government.

It was usually a churchman who was the king's chief minister, or Chancellor. The Chancellor carried out the written and legal business of the kingdom.

When the English tried to take over Scotland, Scottish churchmen fought for their church and country.

1286, King Alexander III

Alexander III was King of Scots from 1249 to 1286. For most of his reign, Scotland was peaceful and prosperous. Alexander's wife was the sister of Edward I, King of England. There were friendly links between the two countries.

Things changed, however, when Alexander's wife died suddenly, leaving no son to be king after him. He married again, the young and beautiful Yolande of Dreux.

On a stormy day in March, 1286, Alexander left Edinburgh Castle to return to his wife at Kinghorn in Fife. He set out to travel the twenty miles by roads and ferryboat across the Firth of Forth.

When Edward I asked Alexander III for homage for Scotland he replied:

'No one has a right to homage for my kingdom of Scotland save God alone, and I hold it only of (from) God.'

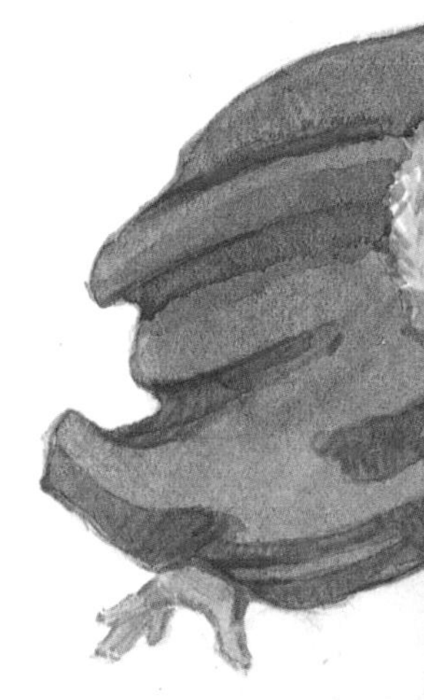

He crossed the Forth safely but by then it was a dark and wild night. He became separated from his companions and next morning was found dead at the foot of a cliff near Kinghorn.

Scotland had lost a strong king. Edward I of England, who had already invaded Ireland and conquered Wales, took this opportunity to try to take control of Scotland.

The Kingdom without a King

When Alexander died, the heiress to the throne was his granddaughter, Margaret, who lived in Norway where her father was king.

Because she was very young, the Scottish nobles chose six guardians to rule the country in her place. Three of them supported the Bruce family and three supported the Balliol-Comyn family. Each of these important families had a strong claim to the throne.

In 1290, Margaret set sail for Scotland but she became ill and died on the journey.

Scotland then had no direct heir to be crowned. Many important lords claimed the throne.

▲ The Guardians of Scotland did not use a king's seal. Their seal showed St. Andrew, patron saint of Scotland.

Norham Castle. Here, in 1291, Edward I wanted to take control of Scotland. The Scots refused him. ▶

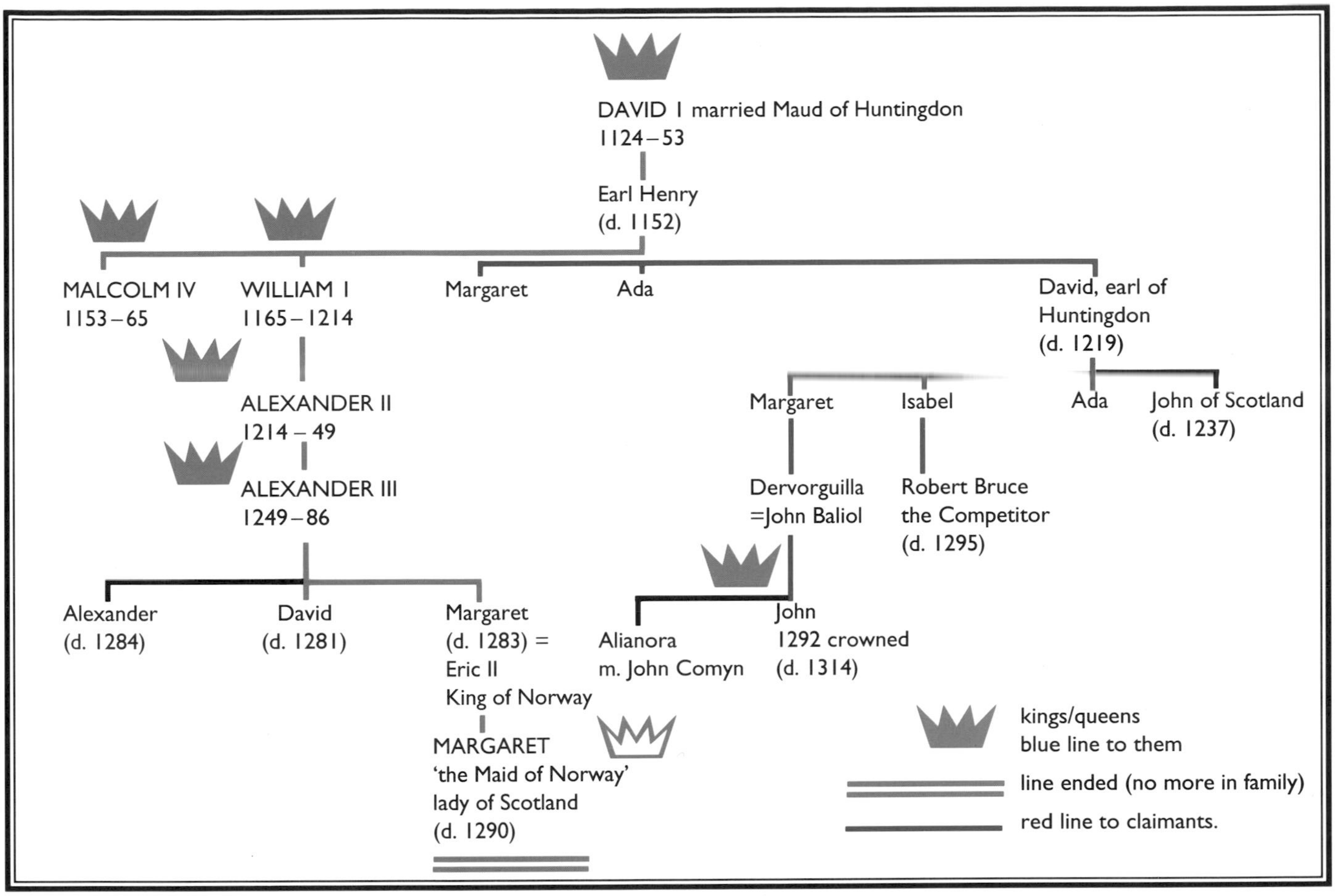

DAVID I married Maud of Huntingdon
1124–53

Earl Henry
(d. 1152)

MALCOLM IV
1153–65

WILLIAM I
1165–1214

Margaret

Ada

David, earl of
Huntingdon
(d. 1219)

ALEXANDER II
1214 – 49

ALEXANDER III
1249–86

Margaret

Isabel

Ada

John of Scotland
(d. 1237)

Dervorguilla
=John Baliol

Robert Bruce
the Competitor
(d. 1295)

Alexander
(d. 1284)

David
(d. 1281)

Margaret
(d. 1283) =
Eric II
King of Norway

Alianora
m. John Comyn

John
1292 crowned
(d. 1314)

MARGARET
'the Maid of Norway'
lady of Scotland
(d. 1290)

kings/queens
blue line to them

line ended (no more in family)

red line to claimants.

When the Scottish lords asked Edward I for help in choosing a king for Scotland, Edward brought his army to the border with him.

Two Scottish nobles had the best claims to the throne. One was the grandfather of Robert Bruce and the other was John Balliol. Edward chose John Balliol who was crowned King of Scots in 1292. He was warned to govern well or Edward would have to interfere.

▲ King John Balliol pays homage to Edward I of England.

England's Warrior King

Edward I was a clever king but he was also a fine soldier. He had conquered Wales and built many strong, stone castles there before turning his attention to Scotland.

His army was made up of heavy cavalry, archers and foot soldiers.

Knights formed the most important part of the English army. A knight wore chain mail armour for protection. So that he could be recognized, he also wore a tunic bearing his own coat of arms. In battle he carried a long lance and a mace or battleaxe. A strong horse was needed to carry the knight, his armour and his weapons during battle.

Edward was ready for war if that was needed to make Scotland part of his kingdom. But the Scots had not fought a war for thirty years.

This is an illustration from 1315 when Robert Bruce attacked Edward I's Carlisle Castle. ▶

◀ King Edward I of England at his coronation in the year 1272.

The Scots army was mainly made up of foot soldiers, called the infantry. Each man wore a helmet and a padded jacket. Chain mail gloves helped him hold a 3.6-metre-long spear. He also carried a tough, leather shield and a sword or dirk (a dagger).

Many Scots nobles owned land in both England and Scotland. They did not know whether to support John Balliol or Edward.

The Bruce family still wanted the throne and remained loyal to Edward.

King John Balliol and the Sack of Berwick

Edward I treated Scotland as if it were a part of England. He tried to force King John to do as he wished. But King John was supported by many of Scotland's churchmen and nobles.

When England went to war with France in 1294, Edward demanded that the Scots fight for him in France. The Scots refused. Instead, they became allies of the French, and King John took his army to the English border.

Edward was furious and took his revenge by attacking Berwick, Scotland's richest town.

Edward I destroyed Berwick to punish the Scots for daring to rebel. ▼

The English soldiers killed, looted and burned for three days. The dead were left in the streets to rot. All Europe was shocked by Edward's behaviour.

The Scots nobles were called to Berwick to sign a document promising loyalty to King Edward I. Otherwise, they would lose their lands.

Edward and his army marched further into Scotland. They took government papers, the crown jewels, holy treasures and the coronation stone (the Stone of Destiny) from Scone.

King John was punished. Edward took from him his tunic, bearing the royal coat of arms, and his knight's belt. As a result, he was nicknamed 'Toom Tabard' (empty jacket). King John was forced to give up his crown.

Scotland no longer had its king, and English soldiers occupied many of the country's important castles.

▲ The Coronation Chair in Westminster Abbey, London. The Stone of Destiny is beneath the throne.

Scots landowners signed the 'Ragman Roll' promising loyalty to Edward I. ▼

The Rise of William Wallace and Andrew Murray

When Edward I believed that Scotland was secure, he returned to England. But the Scots did not accept his rule. Cressingham was Edward's tax gatherer for Scotland. He complained that none of his men could collect money because of threats by the local people.

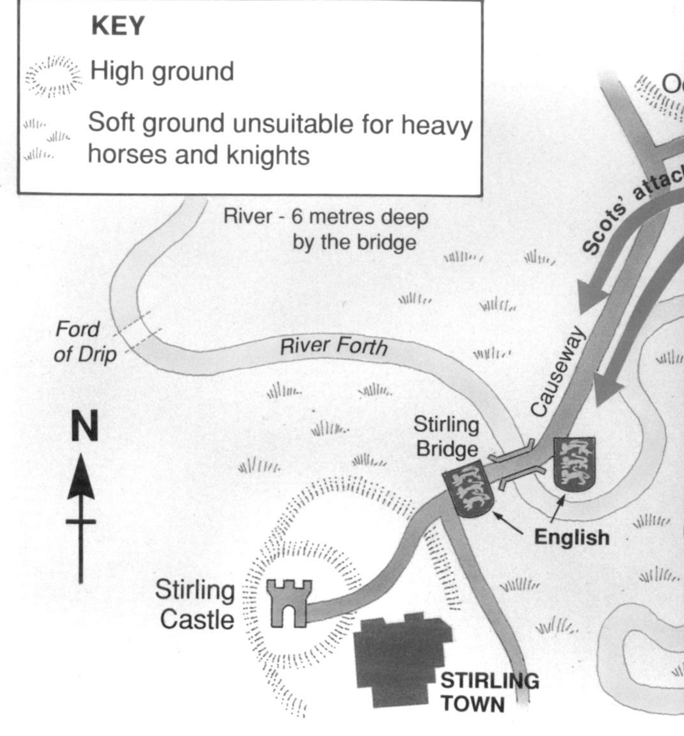

▲ This map shows the Battle of Stirling Bridge, in the year 1297.

Two young men, Andrew Murray in the north and William Wallace in the south, began to collect together armed men. In 1297, they joined forces against the English. Edward sent a strong army to put down this revolt by the Scots. The two armies met at Stirling.

◀ The Wallace Monument stands on Abbey Craig, where Wallace watched and gave orders at the Battle of Stirling Bridge.

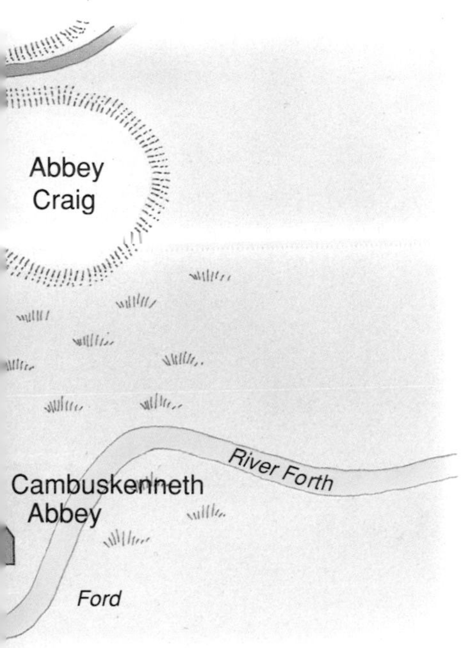

Battle of Stirling Bridge
11 September 1297

The armies faced each other across the River Forth, with the English occupying Stirling Castle. The English were better equipped and confident.

Wallace would not surrender. He said:

'. . . we are not here to make peace but to do battle to defend ourselves and to liberate our kingdom.'

The English leaders argued about how to fight the battle.
Cressingham said:

'Do not waste more of the King's time and money. Cross the river now by the bridge.'

An English knight said:

'Send a force of knights and men to secure the ford. They can attack the Scots from behind and let the rest of our army cross the bridge.'

The English commander, the Earl of Surrey, chose to cross by the narrow bridge. First, the knights on horseback went on to the bridge but, to their surprise, the Scots attacked. The bridge was jammed with horses and men so that the English had no room to fight. Many soldiers were drowned. The English were defeated.

▲ This painting is of the Battle of Stirling Bridge.

Wallace is Defeated

After the Scots victory at Stirling Bridge, Wallace and Murray were made Guardians of Scotland. As Wallace was not a high-born noble, this was a great honour for him.

Unfortunately, Andrew Murray died soon after the battle and Wallace found that few of the important noble families were willing to support him.

Edward hated the Scots even more now, and especially Wallace. He sent a huge army of 4 000 cavalry and 25 000 foot soldiers to Scotland.

▲ 'Bas agus Buaidh - Death and Victory'. Wallace inspired the Scots people and Robert Bruce to fight for freedom even after his death.

The Battle of Falkirk was a disaster for the Scots. The English had better weapons, including the powerful longbow. ▶

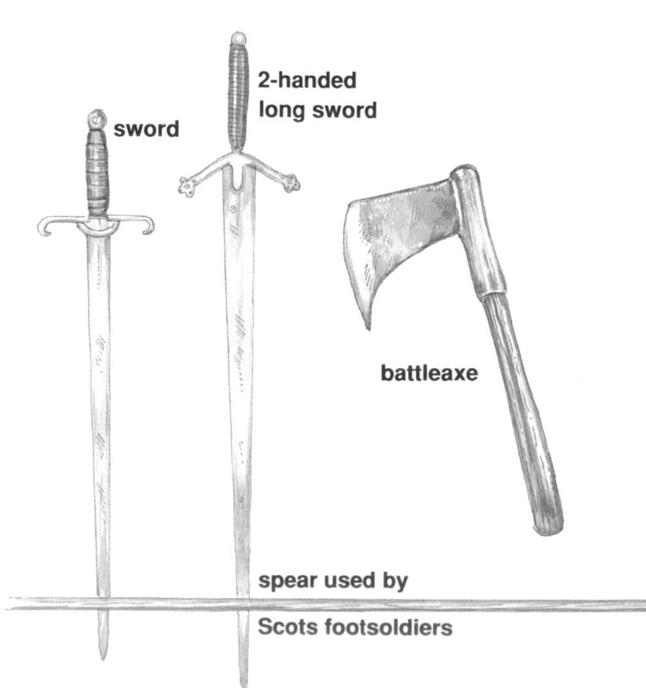

The Scots used the schiltrom, ▶ a 'hedgehog' of spears, to defend themselves against attacks by knights on horseback.

In 1298, the Scots were defeated by this powerful English army at Falkirk. The long Scots spears were no defence against the English longbows which won the battle for the English.

Two of the lords who fought alongside Wallace were John Comyn, nephew of King John Balliol, and Robert Bruce. After the battle was lost, they paid homage to Edward who brought armies to take over even more castles in Scotland.

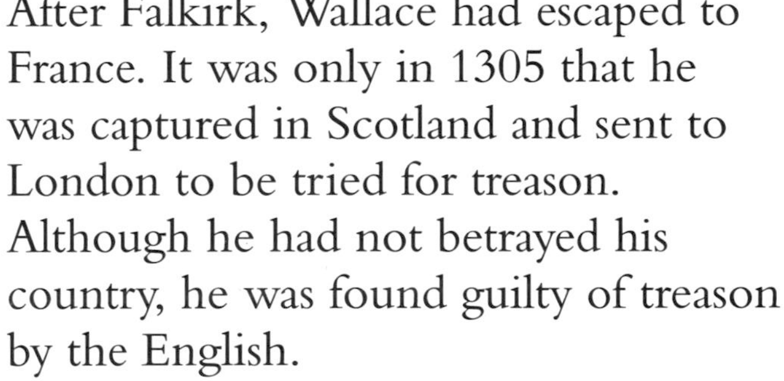

After Falkirk, Wallace had escaped to France. It was only in 1305 that he was captured in Scotland and sent to London to be tried for treason. Although he had not betrayed his country, he was found guilty of treason by the English.

He was hanged, taken down alive, tortured and beheaded. His body was quartered and the pieces sent back to Scotland to frighten the Scots.

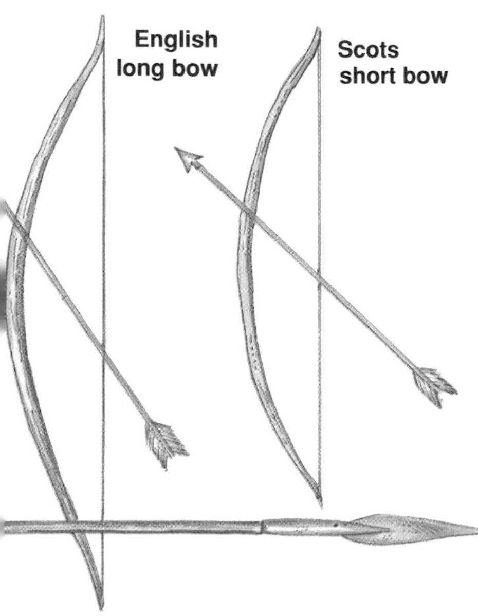

Murder: a Step to the Throne

By 1306, after ten years of fighting, Edward thought that Scotland was safely his. Most nobles and churchmen had promised to serve him rather than lose their lands. But the ordinary people of Scotland and some nobles wanted freedom.

Robert Bruce was Earl of Carrick and Lord of Annandale. He had inherited his family's claim to the throne. He was sure that the people would support a strong king. Bruce had fought alongside Wallace and wanted to be that king.

In Greyfriars Kirk, Dumfries, Bruce met John Comyn, nephew of John Balliol, the last king. Although the two men did not trust each other, it is thought that Bruce had set up the meeting to ask for Comyn's support against the English.

Their meeting ended in a quarrel. Bruce stabbed Comyn, who died. No one knows exactly what happened but this killing, in a church, shocked everyone.

After the murder, Bruce had many enemies. Comyn's family, naturally, were very angry. A furious Edward I began to hunt Bruce down.

▲ Scone Abbey.

The Roman Catholic Church punished Bruce by expelling him.

But Bishop Wishart of Glasgow forgave Bruce and arranged a coronation at Scone Abbey, near Perth. Robert Bruce was crowned and became King Robert I.

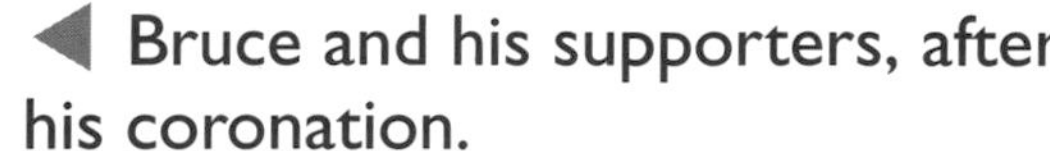

◀ Bruce and his supporters, after his coronation.

Bruce is Defeated and in Despair

The reign of Bruce started badly. After the murder of Comyn, few people trusted him. Edward's armies controlled the land and, three months after his coronation, in 1306, Bruce's small army was destroyed by the English cavalry at Methven, near Perth.

Bruce sent his queen and daughter to Kildrummy Castle and he took to the hills.

As outlaws went they many a day
Among the hills, and fed on meat
And water, nor had else to eat . . .
Thus in the mountains wandered he
Till most men in his company
Were ragged and torn. They had, besides,
No shoes but those they made of hides.

From the poem *The Brus* by John Barbour, written in 1385.

Edward made sure that Bruce's family and friends suffered. Bruce's wife and daughter were captured and locked up in nunneries. His sister, Mary, and the Countess of Buchan (who had crowned Bruce) were kept in cages outside the castle walls of Berwick and Roxburgh. Three of Bruce's brothers were executed. Bishop Wishart was thrown into prison.

▲ Kildrummy Castle was the strongest castle in the north.

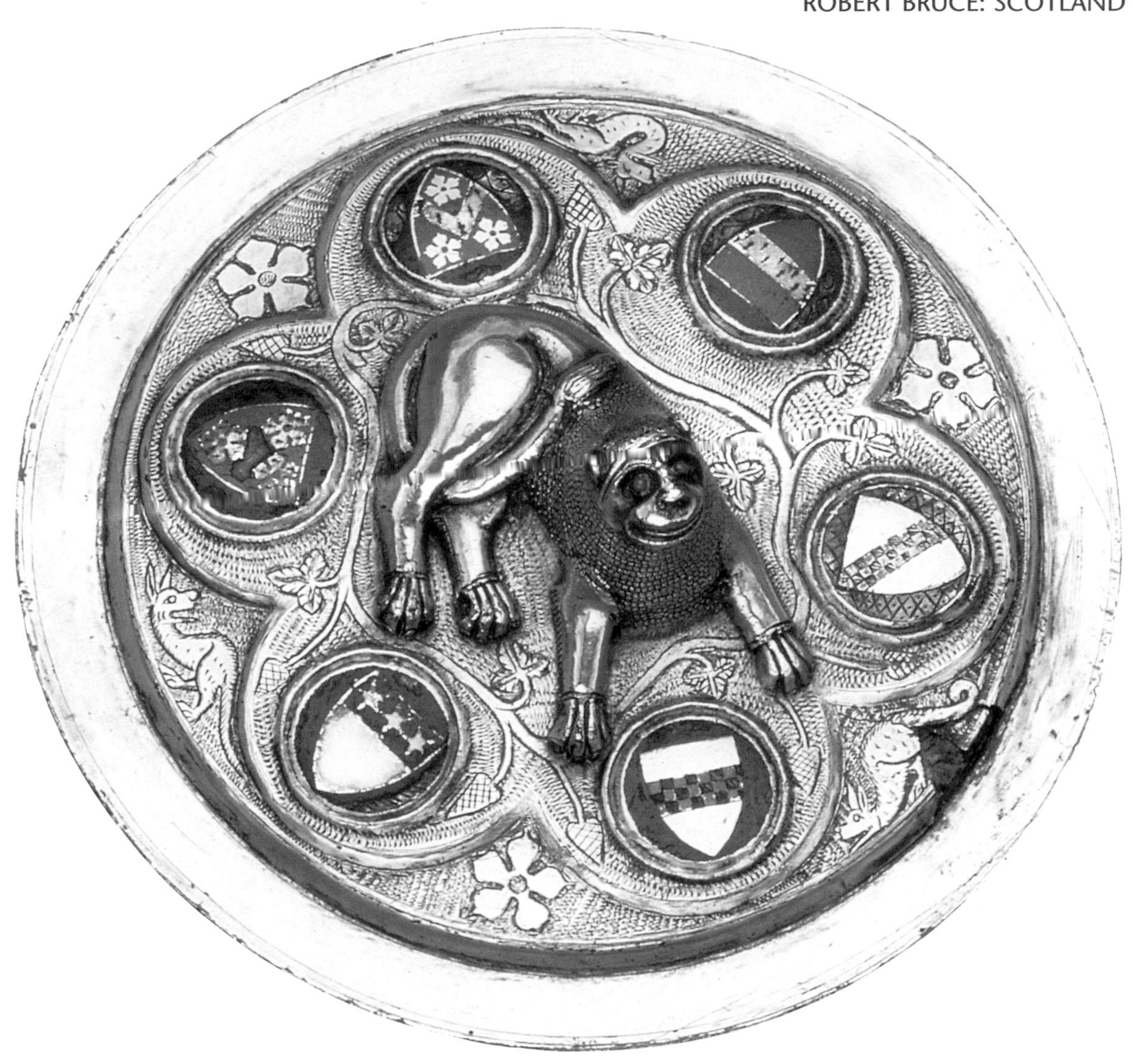

▲ **The lion surrounded by shields on the base of this drinking cup is said to represent Bruce surrounded by his supporters.**

Edward did not catch Bruce, who was helped in the west by loyal supporters like the MacDonalds of Islay.

But when Bruce had news of his family, he must have wondered if the crown was worth all their suffering.

A story is told about Bruce at this time. It is said that, while in despair, he watched a spider trying to complete its web. It failed six times but kept trying. The seventh attempt was a success.

Bruce decided to follow the spider's example. He began to make plans.

Civil War

Bruce landed on the Carrick coast, a place he knew well, to wage a different kind of war. Bruce's orders to his soldiers were to:

- take the English by surprise;
- attack their food wagons;
- make hit-and-run raids;
- avoid big battles and sieges;
- destroy castles so that the English could not use them.

A war of this kind is now called a guerrilla war.

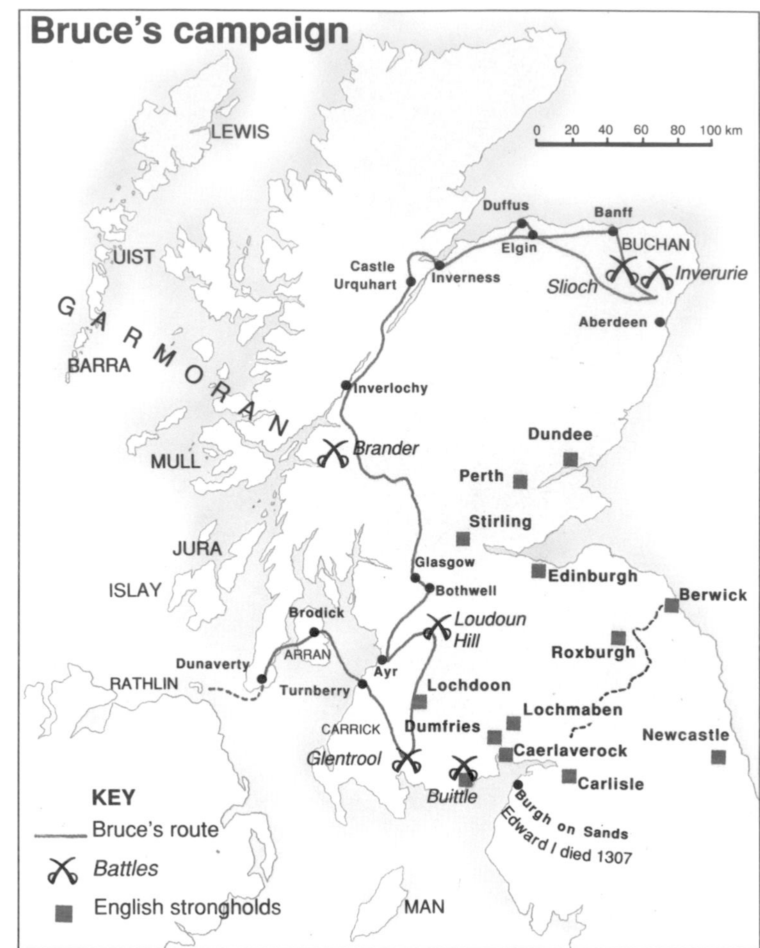

Soon, Bruce had some small successes at Glen Trool and Loudon Hill. In spite of the terrible punishment for Scots who supported King Robert, more and more people came to join him.

◀ Bruce's Stone, Glen Trool.

▲ Bruce ambushed the English in Glen Trool.

In July, 1307, Edward I died on his way north. This was good news for Bruce because Edward's son, now King Edward II, went back to London.

Bruce now set about gaining control of the whole country. He defeated his old enemies, the Comyns, in Aberdeenshire and Moray. At the Pass of Brander, James Douglas defeated the MacDougalls of Argyll, allies of the Comyns.

Bruce's brother, Edward, brought Galloway under control.

King Robert showed he was master of the kingdom by calling a parliament in 1309. He had defeated his enemies. Many of those enemies now supported him because he had shown them mercy.

The Campaign to free the Castles

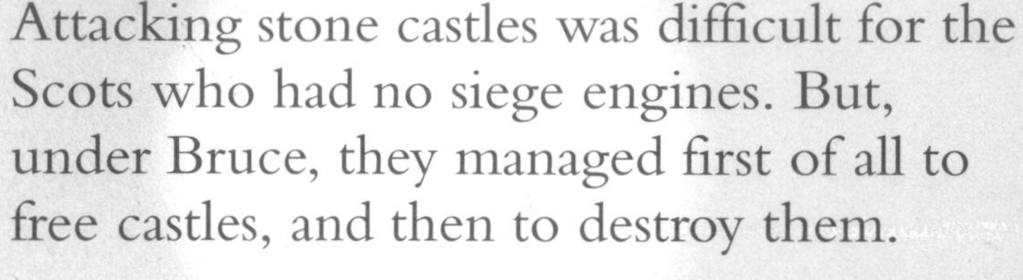

Attacking stone castles was difficult for the Scots who had no siege engines. But, under Bruce, they managed first of all to free castles, and then to destroy them.

Bruce, himself, led the capture of Perth castle by wading through the moat and using a rope ladder to climb the walls.

At Linlithgow, a farmer taking a hay wagon into the castle blocked the portcullis by cutting his horses free. Scots soldiers, hidden in the wagon and in the woods nearby, ran forward to take the castle.

Edinburgh Castle fell to Randolph, Earl of Moray. A local man who knew a secret route led Randolph and the Scots up the steep castle rock and over the walls.

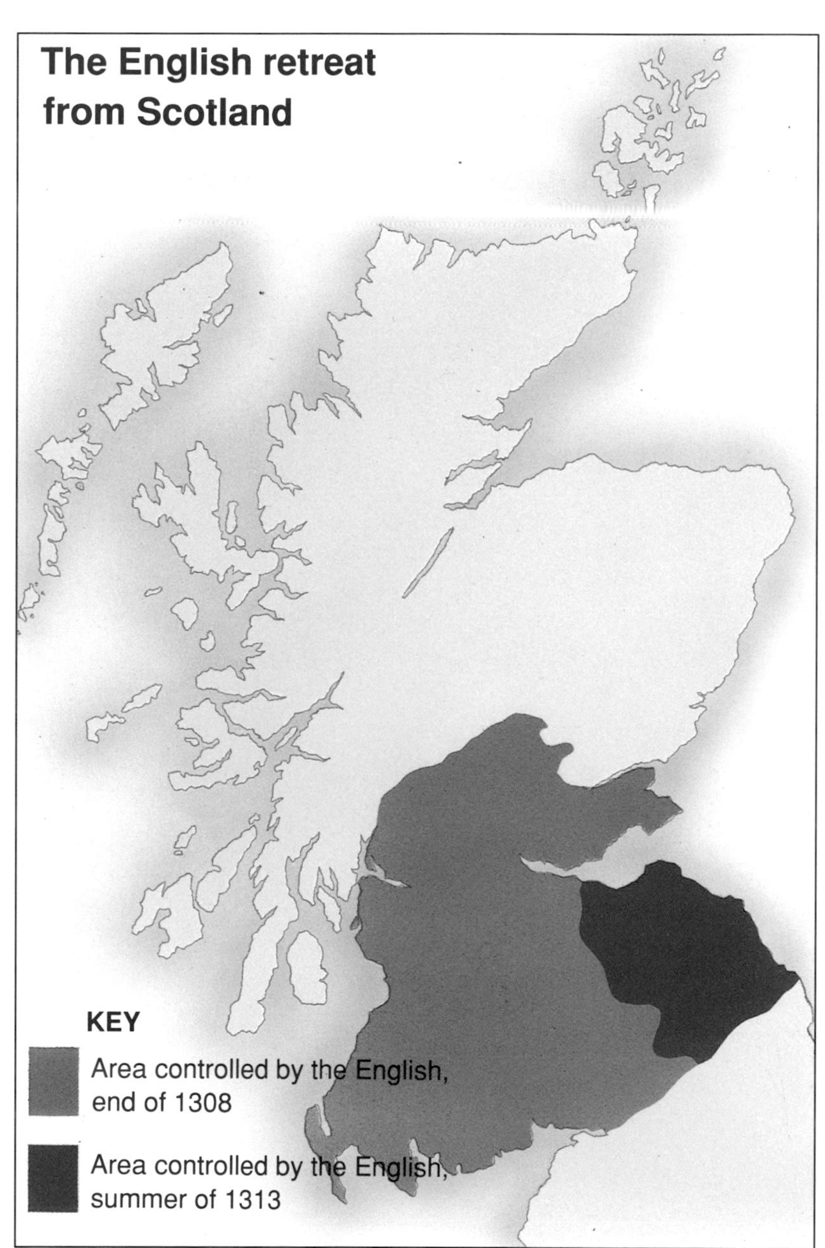

As long as Stirling Castle was held by the English, Scotland could not be free. Bruce's brother, Edward, agreed with the Governor of the castle that it would be handed over to the Scots unless an English army arrived by Midsummer Day, 1314.

King Robert was very angry because he knew that a huge English army would be sent north and he would have to fight.

The Battle of Bannockburn

Edward II was forced to lead an army into Scotland to relieve Stirling Castle. The Scots were greatly outnumbered but had fought successfully for seven years under Bruce.

To prevent the English from reaching Stirling, Bruce chose the battleground carefully. Pits were dug and metal spikes were scattered to make difficulties for the English cavalry.

▲ This fifteenth-century drawing shows Bruce killing Sir Henry de Bohun.

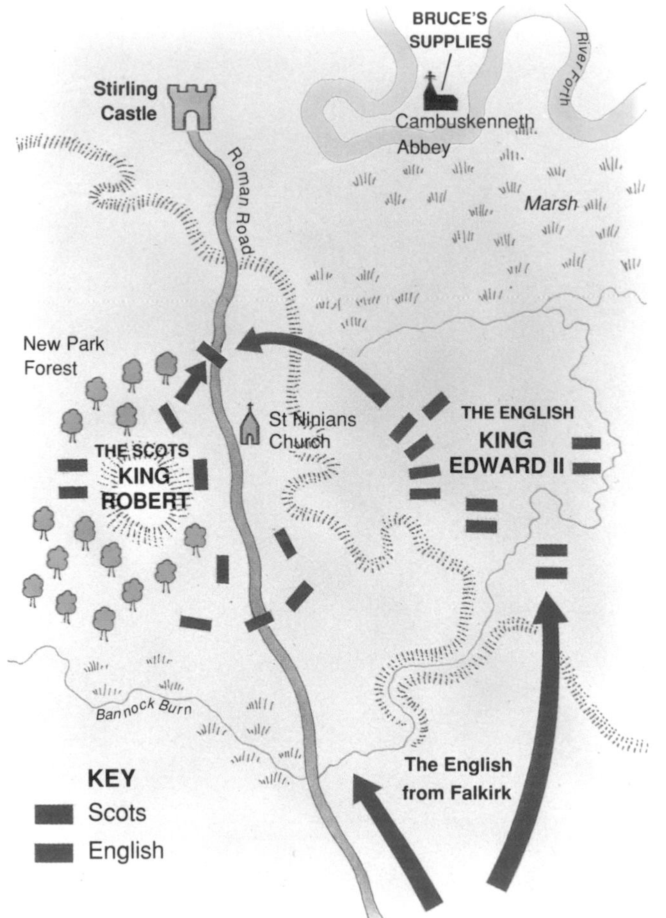

◀ A map of the first day of the Battle of Bannockburn.

As the armies were preparing for battle on 23 June, 1314, an English knight, Sir Henry de Bohun, saw King Robert on a small pony and charged at him with his lance. King Robert killed de Bohun with one blow of his axe. The Scots took courage from the king's bravery.

An English cavalry division tried to surprise the Scots by coming round behind them (see the map opposite) but the spearmen of Randolph's schiltrom advanced and drove them off. Many English knights were killed.

▲ This box containing bones of a Celtic saint was carried by the Scots into battle.

Edward led his army across the Bannock Burn and set up camp. The English spent an uncomfortable night on wet ground surrounded by rivers and marsh.

Next day, 24 June 1314, the Scots spearmen advanced against the mighty English cavalry and gave them no room to charge. The Scots horsemen were used to drive off Edward's archers.

Many English soldiers were pushed into the Bannock Burn and the River Forth. Edward fled from the battlefield to avoid capture.

The English lost heart and began to panic. Many were killed as they rushed to escape. Important prisoners were taken and held to ransom.

Good King Robert

◀ Scottish banks can print their own notes. Bruce and Stirling Castle are shown on this Clydesdale Bank note.

Bruce had won a great battle to prove he ruled all of Scotland. He exchanged his prisoners for the return of his wife, daughter and friends.

He set about forcing Edward II to make peace by sending men in to raid the north of England. There they were paid money to stop them doing more damage. In 1318, Lord James Douglas won Berwick back from England.

To rebuild the country's wealth, people in the burghs were encouraged to trade again.

Three important groups of people helped to run the country. Leaders from the burghs joined nobles and churchmen in King Robert's parliaments.

The church and king made laws which were used for the next 300 years.

After the murder of Comyn, Bruce and his supporters had been excommunicated (put out of the Church) by the Pope. Bruce was a religious man, and he gave money and lands to the Church. Excommunication, therefore, was a terrible punishment.

The Scots sent churchmen and lords with letters to the Pope in Rome to ask him to support Scotland and to help stop the war.

▲ The Seal of King Robert I.

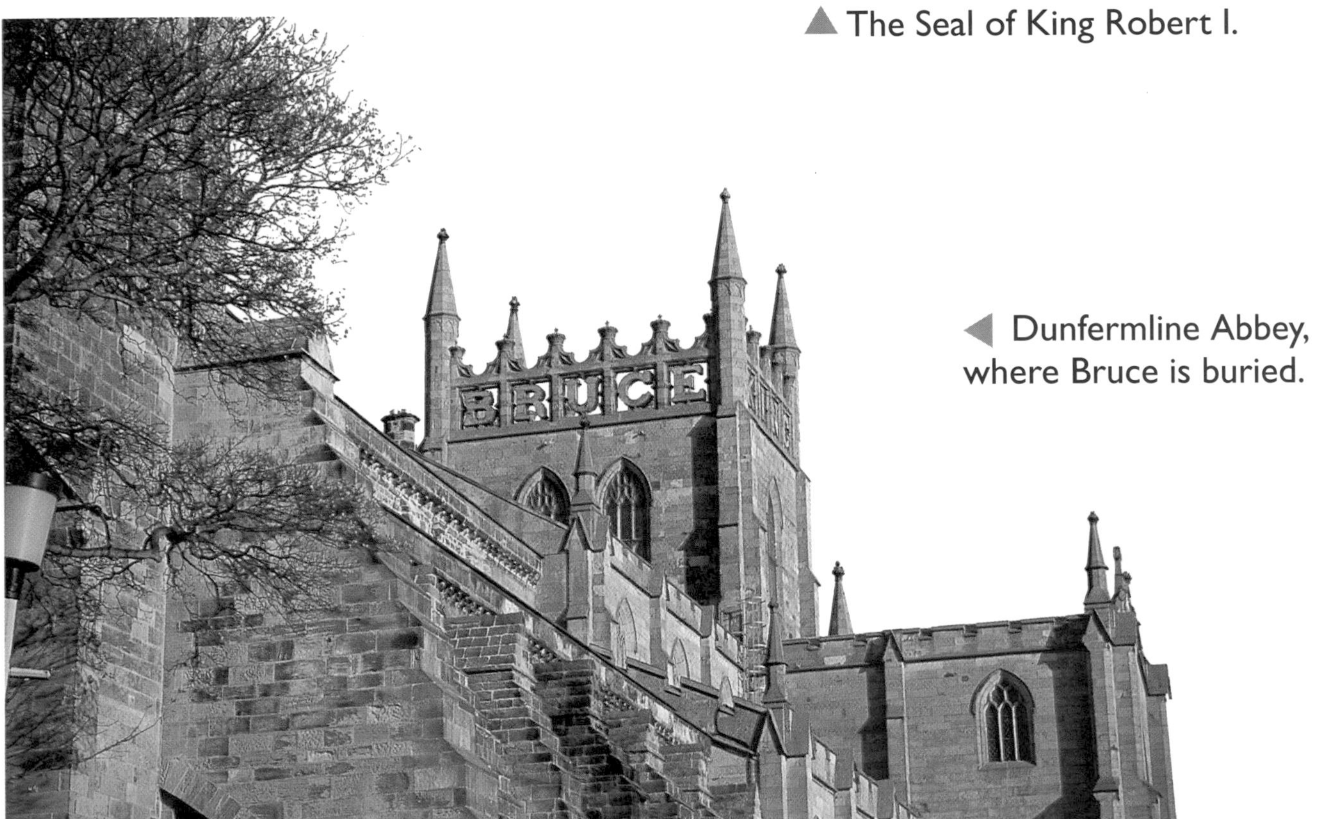

◀ Dunfermline Abbey, where Bruce is buried.

The Declaration of Arbroath

Bruce and his supporters had been expelled from the Church by the Pope. The Scots tried to make the Pope change his mind. Scots churchmen had to obey the Pope's orders but they would not help Edward II.

Leading Scots nobles fixed their seals to a letter sent to Pope John XXII in 1320. They said that they had a right to freedom and a duty to defend it.

The letter asked the Pope to accept that the Scots had a right to defend themselves against their more powerful neighbour, England.

The letter, called the Declaration of Arbroath, said:

> *'For it is not for glory, it is not riches, neither is it honour, but it is freedom alone that we fight and contend for, which no honest man will lose but with his life.'*

The nobles also said that they would never agree to be ruled by the English.

▲ The Declaration of Arbroath.

War between the Scots and the English lasted for several years in spite of the Declaration of Arbroath.

In 1323, the Pope accepted Bruce as King of Scotland. The nation welcomed his heir when, in 1324, Bruce's wife, Queen Elizabeth, gave birth to a son.

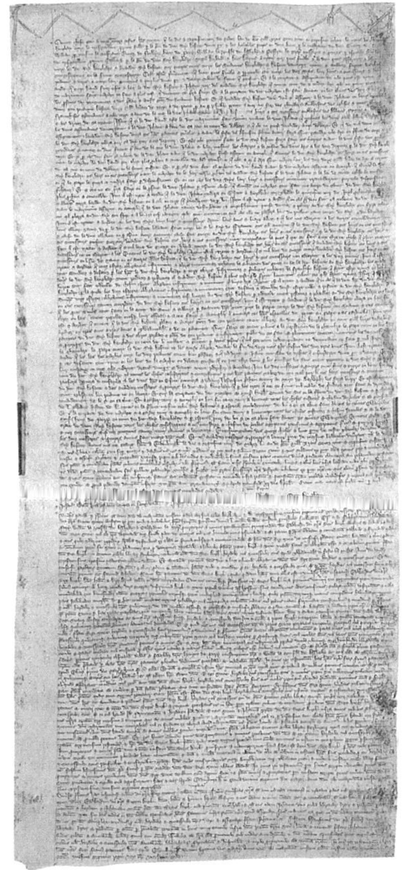

▲ Scotland and England signed this peace treaty in Edinburgh in 1328.

Bruce had proved he was a strong general but also that he was a strong ruler. He had united Scotland.

In 1328, Scotland and England finally signed a peace treaty in Edinburgh. But the English did not return the Stone of Destiny and other items Edward I had taken from Scotland.

◄ Arbroath Abbey, where the Declaration of Arbroath was drawn up.

The Bruce Legacy

Towards the end of his reign, Bruce built a manor house, not a castle, for his home, at Cardross near Dumbarton. He could return here from running his country, to relax and sail his galley.

He had freed Scotland from the English and was finally accepted as King of Scotland by the Pope and by kings of other countries.

Bruce had shown how heavily armoured knights on warhorses could be defeated in battle by well-trained spearmen and by the clever use of a small number of mounted troops in raiding parties.

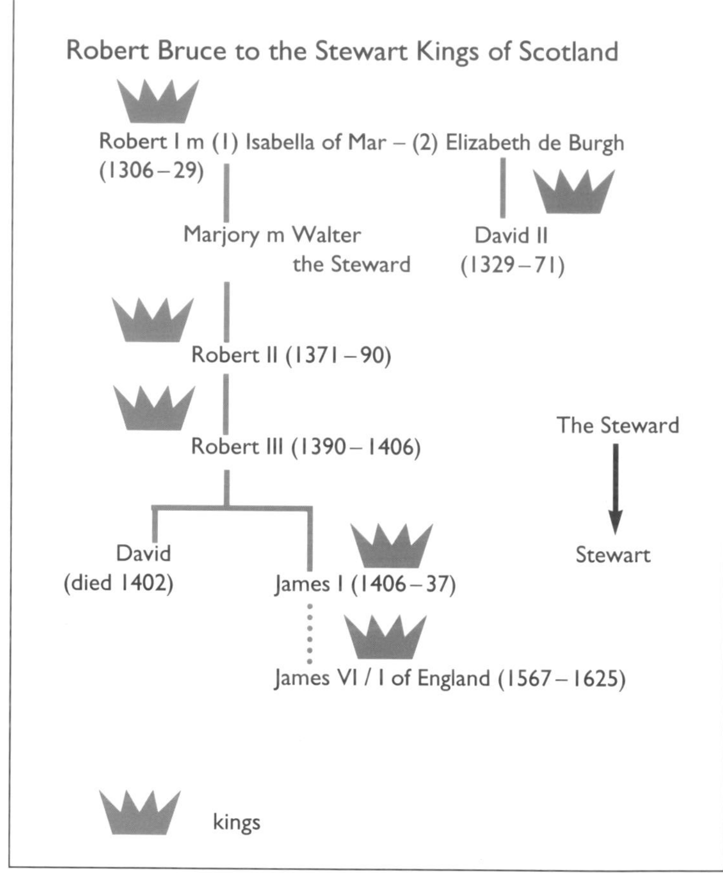

As rewards for loyalty, he gave large areas of land to his supporters, the Douglas, Murray, Stewart and MacDonald families. His enemies were not treated badly, although the Comyns and Balliols were never again allowed to be powerful.

Along with the Church, the nobles and the townspeople played a large part in running the country.

▲ The statue of King Robert I at Bannockburn Heritage Centre.

When Bruce died, his son reigned as David II. David had no children and Bruce's grandson, Robert, became the first Stewart king. Much later, in 1603, the Stewart King James VI brought Scotland and England closer together when he ruled both countries as James VI of Scotland and I of England.

▲ This skull from Dunfermline Abbey is thought to be that of Robert Bruce. It was used by the sculptor for the statue on the opposite page.

Scots Wha Hae

Scots, wha hae wi' Wallace bled,
Scots, wham Bruce has aften led,
Welcome to your gory bed,
Or to victorie!

Now's the day, and now's the hour:
See the front o' battle lour,
See approach proud Edward's power -
Chains and slaverie!

Wha will be a traitor knave?
Wha can fill a coward's grave?
Wha sae base as be a slave? -
Let him turn, and flee!

Wha for Scotland's King and Law
Freedom's sword will strongly draw,
Freeman stand or freeman fa',
Let him follow me!

By Oppression's woes and pains,
By your sons in servile chains,
We will drain our dearest veins
But they shall be free!

Lay the proud usurpers low!
Tyrants fall in every foe!
Liberty's in every blow!
Let us do, or die!

Robert Burns, 1759-96

Wallace and Bruce are great heroes of Scottish history, remembered down the ages in song and story.

The people of Scotland, from the Highlands to the Lowlands, were united by Bruce against a foreign invader, England.

Although wars and battles were to continue for many years, Scotland was safe as a separate nation.

Glossary

Allies People who support you in a war.

Ambushed Made a surprise attack.

Archers Soldiers who used bows and arrows.

Cavalry Soldiers on horseback.

Chain mail Armour made from links of metal.

Galley An open boat with sails and oars.

Guardians People who were chosen to run the country when there was no king.

Guilds Groups of traders or craftsmen who helped each other.

Heir, Heiress Someone who will take a title when the person who holds it dies.

Homage A show of respect or honour to someone.

Looted Stole.

Mace A war club with a metal head, often with spikes.

Middle Ages A name given to the time in history between 500 and 1500 AD.

Missionaries People who moved around the country spreading their religious beliefs.

Orders (religious) The different groups of monks and nuns.

Portcullis A gate that can be lowered to close an entrance to a castle.

Ransom A price paid to free a prisoner.

Sack Stealing, destroying and killing throughout a city, usually by soldiers.

Schiltrom A company of spearmen packed together in a circle, with spears pointing outwards.

Siege engine A machine for attacking castles by firing stones at them.

Tolls Payments for the use of something, such as a road or a mill.

Touns Small groups of farm houses.

Treason Betraying your country.

Picture acknowledgements
The publishers wish to thank the following for providing the illustrations in this book: British Library 17; The Master and Fellows of Corpus Christi College, Cambridge 15, 34; Crown copyright/By permission of the Controller of Her Majesty's Stationery Office 21 (bottom), 39; Cumbria Record Office 19; Donald Gunn 30, 31; Historic Scotland 13 (both), 27, 28, 37 (left), 39; National Galleries of Scotland/Scoular 41; © The Trustees of the National Museums of Scotland 29, 35; By permission of the Duke of Roxburghe/National Library of Scotland 7 (top); Scottish Record Office 38; Still Moving Picture Company 7 (bottom, A Burgess), 22 (left, K Paterson), 40 (Alasdair Smith); Wayland Picture Library 18, 37 (right); By courtesy of the Dean and Chapter of Westminster 21 (top); David Williams Picture Library 12, 16 (bottom).
Artwork by: Peter Bull 6, 8, 10, 22-3, 24-5 (bottom), 30, 33, 34; Chris Ryley 9, 14-15, 20, 25 (top), 26, 32; Royal Arms of Scotland on cover and title page by John Yates.
Thanks to Professor Charles W J Withers for the languages map references on page 6.

A map of Scotland, including places mentioned in the text.

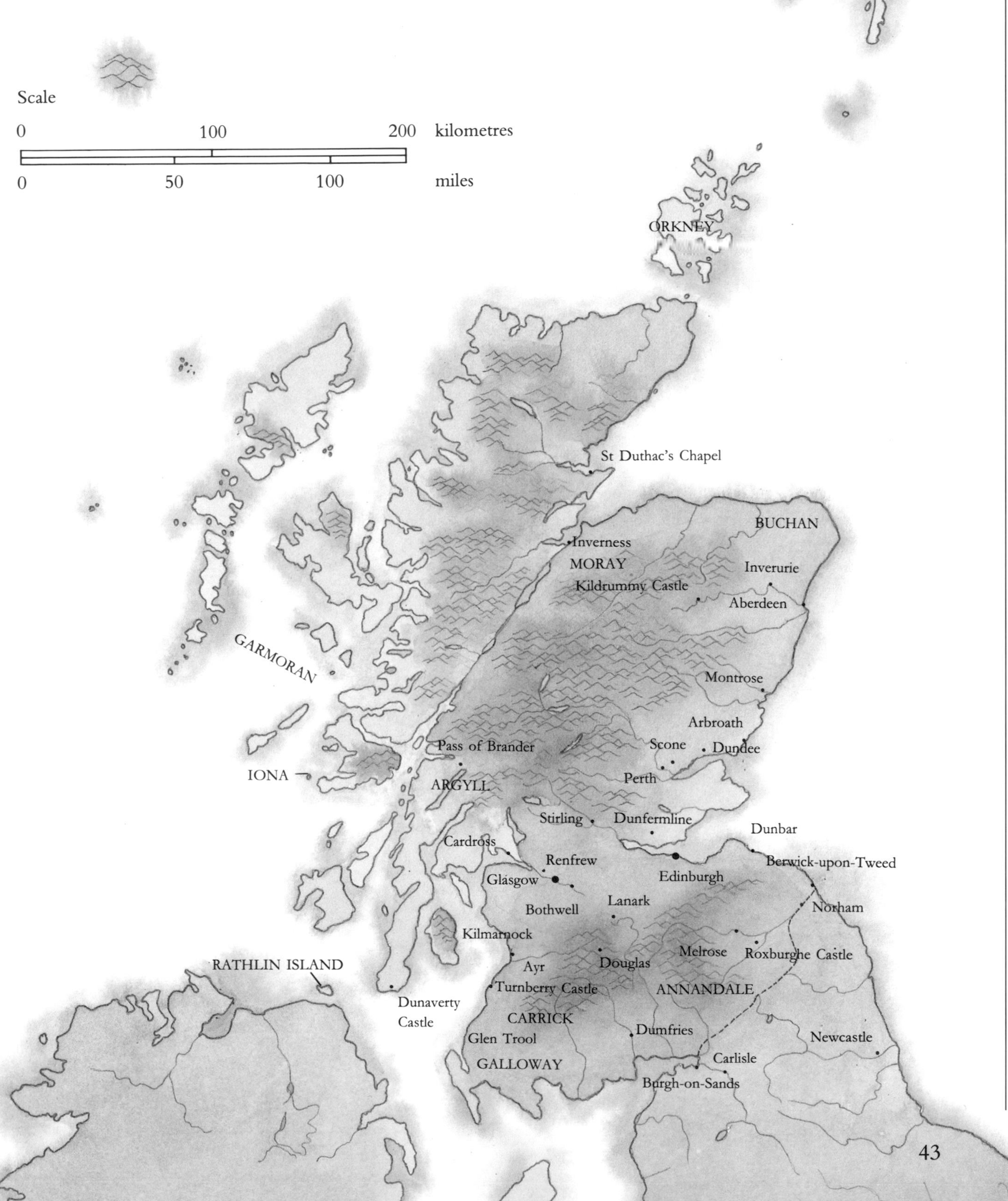

Further Information

Books to read

Non fiction:

Some history books give information on Scotland as well as England at this time or the information is suitable to both countries.

Norman Britain by Tony Triggs (Wayland, 1990). A good general picture of the Normans.

History Makers of the Middle Ages by Peter Chrisp (Wayland, 1994). Includes a chapter on Robert Bruce.

Robert the Bruce, King of Scots by Ronald McNair Scott (Canongate Press, 1988).

Fiction:

Quest for a Maid by Frances Mary Hendry (Canongate Press, 1988).
A story of people in the burghs at the time of the death of Alexander III.

Places to visit

Bannockburn Heritage Centre run by National Trust for Scotland.
Wallace Monument run by Stirling District Council.
Scottish Abbeys and Castles - many are run by Historic Scotland, who produce guide books. Historic Scotland also produce good packs of information on many historic places such as Arbroath Abbey and Stirling Castle.
There are often local references to the Wars of Independence around the country. Museums and maps are good starting points to find out more.

BBC Education Scotland have produced the following two units of programmes on this topic:
For TV – *Bruce's Scotland* in *Around Scotland.*
For radio – *Wallace's Scotland* in *Scottish Resources: 10-12.*
Print support is available from: BBC Education Scotland, 5 Queen Street, Edinburgh EH2 1JF.

Index

Numbers in **bold** refer to illustrations as well as text.

Arbroath, Declaration of **38-9**
armies
  English 17, 18, 21, **22**-3, 24-5, 28, **33, 34**-5
  Scottish 9, 19, 20, **23**, 25, 28, **34**-5

Balliol, King John *see under* kings of Scotland
Balliol-Comyn family 16, **17**, 25, 31, 40
Bannockburn, Battle of **34**-5
Bohun, Sir Henry de **34**, 35
Bruce, Alexander 13
Bruce, Edward 31, 33,
Bruce, Robert 6-7, 25, 26, 27, 28-9, 31, **37**, 39-**41**
  acceptance by Pope 39, 40
  birth 6
  coronation 27
  excommunication from Church 27, 37, 38
  family 6-7, 9, 10, 17, 19, 26, 28, 29
  fight against English 25, 28, **30**-36
  murder of John Comyn 27, 37
  supporters **29**, 30, 31, 38, 40
Brus, The (extract) 28
burghs 10-11, 36
  Aberdeen 11
  Annan 10
  Berwick 11, 20-21, 28, 36
  Perth **10**

castles **8**, 9, 10, 18, 21, 25, 30, 32-3
  Edinburgh 14, 33
  Kildrummy **28**
  Linlithgow 33
  Perth 32
  Roxburgh **11**, 28
  Stirling 23, 33, **34**, **36**

Celtic Church 12
civil war 30-31
Comyn, John 25, 27
Cressingham 22, 23
crown jewels 21

Douglas, James 31, 36

England 6, 7, 9, 11, 14, 15, 19, 20, 36, 39, 41
Europe 11, 12, 21

Falkirk, Battle of 24, 25
Forth, River **23**, 35
France 20, 25

Glen Trool **30-31**
Guardians of Scotland **16**, 24
guilds 10

horses 9, 18, 23, 35, 40

Ireland 6, 15

kings of England
  Edward I 14, **16**, **17**, **18**-19, 20-21, 22, 24, 25, 26, 27, 28, 29, 31, 39
  Edward II 31, 34, 35, 36, 38
  James I 41
kings of Scotland 9, 10, 13
  Alexander III 8, 11, 14-15, 16
  David I 6-**7**, 12
  David II 41
  James VI 41
  John Balliol **17**, 19, 20-21, 25, 27
  Robert I *see* Bruce, Robert
  Robert II 41
knights 7, **9**, 18, 21, 23, **25**, 35, 40

languages **6**-7
  Gaelic 6
  Inglis 6
  Norman-French 6-7
  Scots 6

Loudon Hill 30

MacDonalds of Islay 29, 40
MacDougalls of Argyll 31
Margaret of Norway 16
monks 12
Murray, Andrew 22, 24

Normans 6-7

parliaments 31, 36
populations 9

Ragman Roll **21**
Randolph, Thomas, Earl of Moray 33, 35
Roman Catholic Church 12, 27, 37, 38-9

schiltroms **25**, 35
Scone Abbey **27**
Scottish Church 12-13, 20, 38, 40
  and government 13
Stewarts **40**, 41
Stirling Bridge, Battle of **22-3**, 24
Stone of Destiny **21**, 39

touns 8
trade 10-11, 36

Wales 15, 18
Wallace, William 22, 23, **24**-5, 26, 41
war 18, 20, 22-3, 24-5, 26, 30-31, 32-3, 34-5, 39, 41
weapons 9, 18, **24-5**
Wishart, Bishop of Glasgow 27, 28